MUSIC FOR E

To McDonalD

from Brian

with much gratitude

Music For Brass

BRIAN WALTHAM

PETERLOO POETS

First published in 1990
by Peterloo Poets
2 Kelly Gardens, Calstock, Cornwall PL18 9SA, U.K.

British Library Cataloguing in Publication Data
Waltham, Brian
    Music for brass.
    I. Title
    821.914

    ISBN 1-871471-20-6

Printed in Great Britain by
Latimer Trend & Company Ltd, Plymouth

ACKNOWLEDGEMENTS

'My Father' was first published in *The Listener*.

'Insomniacs Inc.' and 'Survivor' were first published in *Poetry Matters*.

'Transit' was published in *Poems Of Place* (Mandeville Press, 1986).

'It Was Always Here' was published in *Weyfarers 37* (Guildford Poets Press, 1983)

'Home' won the £100 4th prize in the 1988 *Peterloo Poets Open Poetry Competition*.

'Insomniacs Inc.' won the £200 3rd prize in the 1989 *Peterloo Poets Open Poetry Competition*.

Twelve poems in the present collection appeared in *Peterloo Preview 1* (1988).

This volume was produced with assistance from the Ralph Lewis Award at the University of Sussex.

Contents

Transit

Motoring on country roads you still see them;
Half a mile of wall, stone gateway crested in a statement,
Parkland, beeches and paddocks, the right cattle,
Woods arranged as furniture and somewhere the house.

And somewhere the years, rough headstone and
Family vault, the owning and the owned,
Death come easy and the beautiful children.
Those who owned the seasons, tenanted winter,
Let the primrose happen and the Maundy money,
Or called in tithes across the parchment.
Those who gleaned in the furrows or
Stood dumb at the font or waited like the hare
For Advent, Easter, the Sundays after Trinity,
Or sat idle in the fume of a hedge or
Scythed away time in the Anglican sun.

Those who never left and, as you never will be,
In this place were once at home
And are not dismissed as you change gear
Wondering what it is used for now.

Insomniacs Inc.

We're a quiet lot,
Cunning at exit from a bed, knowing
Blindfold where the furniture is,
Good at doors and floorboards,
Abseiling the stairs, heating like
Night-nurses our four o'clock cuppers.
Cat-burglars in our own rooms, we
Skirt the moonlit sideboard, hear
An ambulance two miles away or a
Bird that's got the time wrong or the
Maddening snores of the righteous.

A prey to all that is terminal, we
Study the hills and plains of a
Crumb on the kitchen table, we grasp
Einstein, re-fight Waterloo and lose,
Count the next ten breaths, become
Inoperable, lie in the oven-bound coffin,
Decide not to buy a new pair of shoes.

For all this we have nothing to show,
No wounds, nothing to say this side
Of dreaming, that side of waking:
A mild attack of death, of no interest
To the reborn others who grind coffee
And are ready for the day.

Home

If you really want to know,
It was wet shale and granite,
Ruts that could break a cart,
Tilted bogland, sheep against walls,
A learner's watercolour with unfinished
Trees and the hilltops not attempted.
It was blanked-off villages, stone
And slate, chapel for the dying and
Up at the crossroads the same few
Names, the rain-washed men of the Somme.
It was simply that place, made that way,
An old sodden coat, handed down,
Lived in, known in every thread.
If you really want to know,
Go there as homecoming,
See yourself tethered like a house,
Arms spread out for trouble like
The place you were born in.

My Father

Courteous in death as in life,
It seemed that he stepped back
And indeed like a courtier in a dark hall
Stepped back shedding detail, a last kindness
To blur away the focus.
And so it is these years later
That I think of goodness with no eye to detail,
A trick of light among shade and sun.

A Kind of Seeing

From the inward fold, from loss of giving,
From all winter protect me.
Rain in the night and now a wind
Ruffling the bright puddles with ideas,
Belfries and office blocks swaying paper-thin
And memory of other water, leaf-coloured near a lane
Or seen lazy through the poppies of Delos
And things said once for all.
Teach me at least boundaries,
Ways to put a mark and turn for home.

Requiem

In this pub awake for the creation
A wake for the cremation God help me
Leaning at the bar half pissed among
The keening of his friends and
Like a war they're saying staying
Your brother your own brother lived
Out good and bad to where they snap
And had us laughing in the trenches.
And sure enough above ground still around
For another round this was his regiment
And three fingers of the spirit the
Lord be with it drinking like Adam
Before the fall and better by Christ
Than the hospital tray of his things
And eight minutes of laundered tremulo
Chapel-in-the-valley as you watch it go
Or a room with his debt, regret, bedwet
In it and get well soon and die in it.

XVIth Century Gallery

Walked in for the greatness
And saw one slim back.
Slimmed great in the oneness
And saw back for the walk.

Solemn-dawdled, rushed three
Crucifixions, two popes,
Crossed on tiptoe hooves to
Stand behind at her pieta
Suffering beyond its glass.

Angels and altars, back of warm neck,
Bits of florid heaven, Jesus dead as anything,
Hair tumbling to a neat collar, mirrored nose,
Cotton shoulder bracing holy feet,
Hair-smell, haloes, curve of cheek and
She now aware of goat breath and
One too many ghosts among the cherubim.

It would be nice to say that we spoke
And that Caravaggio brought us together.
Well, no. She moved away and what with
Religion and the attendant on his stool
I just clopped off across the marble.

August

We sit in the blank heat
Discussing what love might be
If love were love, she in a skirt
With buttons down the front:
And this, from long practice, would
Be easy but that in green beyond her
Head I see arms flung out in passion
Once for all, leaves that turn their
Thighs to the sun, flowers rank with
Midday lust, every button undone.

In Any Case

Including that day at Upperfield
When thunder made us run for the barn
And the high unshouldered door with
The sun still on it and inside the
Church-like creaking and tractor oil,
The ladder against bales and the first
Huge raid on iron close above us.

Not exactly then, you understand,
But in that hollow under
The wood where a barn would be
Had she been there
And there had been thunder.

Or again our fumbling need and
The wrong words and gaucherie
On our raincoat bed.
In any case, now or sometime as
We lie here, the weeping rust,
The urgent smell of straw and under
Our clerestory the tap-tap on an oil drum
Will be as they may be
This side of wonder.

And I swab her bike-saddle
With my shirt while the hedge flames,
A cloud runs to fox the stubble and
Confound that oak, then or in any case
This other side of thunder.

Almost

I was almost there, almost lived it,
That childhood under the elms echoing
With laughter on a summer evening
Safe near the sunlit gables.
I almost remember us, the loose gathered
Family, our secrets and the private words,
My first pony in the sloping paddocks,
The treetop castles and my high attic bed.
Almost I can bear bravely the ruin and
Selling up and sad farewells to the servants,
Safe always in what cannot be taken away
From the years I almost had.

Alchemy

When, for a time, the two of you
Are first on Earth who ever loved,
Beware what things you touch.
Such secrets in your hands then
As move the galaxies
And Midas never guessed at.
The fire inheres in the least of things.
In a plate or a chair you may see
Your own truth half a lifetime later.

Archive

In my file she is eighteen,
Rapier slim, keen on tapestry,
Face not yet written on and
Won't let me because she
Wants to be a nun.

Her own file deals briefly with a
Nervous talker, might become a priest,
Might take ascetic vows, but would
Like to try it once at least.

Meeting, middle-aged, over squares of cheese
At that sort of party, we smile open-ended
And though nothing much is said,
Agree to leave our records unamended.

Doubts About a Painting

The equipment looks fine:
Horse, dog, laced-up wife, doll children
And behind him fifty yards of house and
Holding it all together, an eye that says mine.

Extras, just off the frame, and allowed
To stand up straight for a minute,
Are you and me with our yokel faces.

In our muddled peasant way
We seem to remember thinking it's
Getting late for this sort of thing
As we turn and bend back to our reaping.

Club Class

This runway, feathery tarmac
Flagged up by the moon,
We sink through without harm
And Earth has a claim on us
In our own print, a grid of light,
Sodium groves and crescents,
A high street, an insect roundabout.
And for all the one-off chances,
The finger-tip deals and foreign dust,
Our debts grow as buildings gain height.
Among memos and restaurant bills
We search for someone we can land
With his own key to faces and a
Corgi toy and his own weight.

Samoa

But in that January heat, that
Garlanded plenty, I would want
An east wind at the stile,
The noise of bare branches,
Grass with frost in it,
Ice on the spinney weir and
Hills crouched like bony cattle.

By your leave, I would want
An awkward northern wooing,
Aimed-off shyness, a fallow distance,
Even a thorn hedge of pride
And, like the slow land,
An April worth the winning.

Survivor

Eating machine with clockwork eyes
Strut-waddling like a maddening toy
And all the colour of five days dead,
Scavenge thing, belfry spoiler, berry gobbler,
Mindless flapping shit dispenser,
Carrier of messages that can only be bad,
Ubiquitous, unlovable, unkillable pigeon.

Whether spy from the off-white kingdom
We shall not be here to know. But in
Concrete waste and not another creature living
Be sure he will be here, scratching at banknotes,
Briefcases, photographs, spectacles,
Peering witless at the copper sky.

Heigh Ho

Down at heel busker,
Coal-shiny coat and tail
Poncing it on your telly aerial,
Tuning your strad, thirds and
Seventeenths, throw-away harmonics,
A heart-throb vibrato and suddenly
Your four-note vent of lust and
Twice for luck and from nowhere
Mocking in and out of key
A heigh ho strut, an arc of nothing
But notes, a daft trill, runs two
Octaves above the possible, a yell
From the slums, tone-deaf ornaments,
Notes anyhow, a virtuoso shambles;
And all touch and go, all for
Right here and now, with one mad eye
Cocked for love and enemies.

Sunday School Treat

All things bright and clammy
Grass under canvas, the vicar with
His special voice and all things
Watch the beat, sandwiches bright
And beautiful we musn't yet have
And Miss Webb watching and tall Sir
To give away the prizes.
All things wise and lifebuoy soap
And Jenn with her cough and Sam
With his wasted leg and all
Creatures and daft Fred puzzling
At the raindrops and watch the
Beat wise and wonderful.

The Less Clear Endings

The less clear endings,
They too need the clump of earth
And a keening angry wake.
The less clear love, less clear
That didn't quite reach,
The unborn like elderly dwarfs,
The limping retreat, faith lost
By the inch and vision smeared away,
Oh let them too, these walking wounded,
Have a blunt stop of breath, an end
Worth the name, a grave worth digging.
And right, wrong, anyhow we'll see them out
With an all-night of quarrel and shouting
And tears and purging laughter.

Sandman

I had forgotten him,
Uncle Nothing dressed up in a cloak,
Beckoning from the curtain fold,
So waggish and familiar I never
Thought he went to other rooms.
It was a secret and
His jokes were easy as sleep.

Now in this doorway
The same fever smell,
Daytime sounds from the street
And there on the bed
One who watches the curtain fold
And smiles.

Action

Take last night, for instance.
The right setting, a lovely build-up,
Well-aimed cameras missing nothing,
This hungry girl arched over me
Remembering every word of the script,
And there am I, sole audience and critic,
Thinking: 'the part calls for a younger man',
Or even—for I make jokes in my dreams—
'The man calls for a younger part'.

Petit Mal

To meet a dream at midday, not willingly,
But lurched into the mind with an
Intimate grin like a nightclub friend
And sick again to travel again in a
Fairground bucket the rim of the bearable,
Idiot tunnel, tinsel slope, fear decked
Out in colours, misery of the newborn
And the very old and all of it with
Guilt that you wear like a hand.

This, like nothing I know, will make
Me pray for things I can touch, ordinary
Sounds, questions that have an answer,
A friend or two.

Maison de Vacances

Doors with a grudge, a book open where it was left,
Last year's woodsmoke, another fall of plaster,
A damp patch, shutters that will not budge;
House, you're in a sulk like a neglected girl.

Come, we'll light a fire, such a fire,
And you shall show me your winter trophies;
Fly husks in shabby webs, a shrivelled mouse,
Moths and wasps in their window graveyard.

After the Tempest

It seems he suddenly called it quits,
Went back well-heeled to Stratford,
Had a house built, became a Burger,
Fought one or two law suits
And married off his daughter.

And there we leave him, a retired
Chap like others, worried about the thatch,
Arguing over a dowry and, although wordy,
A useful voice on the drainage committee.

Too Much Wildlife

Stooped over the morning and surely
Aware of talons on his shoulder,
He stands by my desk.
All three of us are anxious
Not to say the wrong thing.
I do not notice as it craps
Down his jacket and strops its beak
In strands of hair combed forwards.

How different with Bagshott who
Breezes in, expansive, wearing as usual
A friendly cobra round his neck.
        'I'm sure you can't have forgotten,
        But don't you agree it would
        Be ridiculous if . . . '
He laughs and I laugh and each of us
Laughs at the other laugh, while the
Mongoose yawns awake in my lap.

Song

Do you hear them, the clamorous dead,
Convicts in a shuffling tread,
Questioning the clocks, in broad day crying
To walk again among the dying?

Shut beyond birth and birth
They reach for things of earth,
To touch with hands again
The warm face of hope and pain.

For all the grief
They found their stay too brief
And ask for breath to draw
One last time more.

At a Meeting of the Hamburg Rückversicherungsgesellschaft

Well, why not?
It's *my* nose
And I bet you have worse habits.

Let's agree that when the dam bursts,
Head slopping in green misery,
Then crude blasting, primitive technology
Has its place.

But for the drier nose
Rich with limpet nodules
God has given us cunning fingers.

Mornings are best
—premier cru—
Thoughtful and difficult.
Good for the hands too,
Keeping alive old potter skills,
Kneading and rolling, in
Direct touch with the material.

Evenings, the little finger only,
Are more austere, but excellent
Practice in timing and patience.

Disposal is a problem
Especially in a bare room
(flicking, in my view, should
be left to the superbly skilful)
But preferable surely to that rancid
Rag stuck to the lining of your pocket?

Planning Ahead

Please do not think me ungrateful
And certainly, as lives go, this is a good one,
But in my next can I please play the B minor fugue
In the Thomaskirche?
If that is fully booked, could I join the queue for being
Tall enough and bronzed enough and languid enough
To cope with tall bronzed languid girls?
If that is unavailable, could I perhaps have two or three
Small daughters, practical but graceful on the deck
Of my yacht, or if that is difficult, just one
To paddle my second-hand rubber dinghy?

The Way It Is

Is it surprising we
Couldn't give that much again
Or with others make it new,
Nor me nor you?
It can happen that words
Answer to what we are
And given means given.

We are each other's bounds,
A space that is us.
Small makes it small
And one smile, with what
There can be in one smile,
Is lethal voltage in the fence
Or suddenly can redeem
The borrowed millions.

Radio 3

Look, Bach, I'm sorry to switch you off,
But only God is allowed to go on being
Right all the time in detail and in sum
And then say it all twice, back to front,
Upside down and get it right again.
Once for all, you are totally absolutely
Endlessly right. You are fundamentally
Finally right.
Now will you please shut up.

Snatch

Outside Selfridges
Propped nude against a van,
She held out beseeching arms.

For her folly they lugged her off
Horizontal, stiff with shock.

Changing clothes with the seasons,
She comes to the window as I pass.

For her folly they put her with
Men in beachwear, green wellies,
Cocktail suits, leisure bargains,
Ascot loungers, men about town
And now, as she stares at me,
With a swine in a dressing gown.

Wasp and Cloudfaces

Tail spin apple-drunk to my bare chest
On a day between weathers, storm-washed.
Hillside quick in and out of sun and
Cumulus in a hurry, lording it sharp edged.

Revs up, stalls and like me stares at
The changes, ogre to saint, king to
Bubbly fool, heroes trapped in rock,
Rootless thinkers, the gaunt lover
Turning from his ageing girl.

Slews into wind on his hairy runway,
Taxies crab-wise round a nipple
And yaws off an inch above a thistle.

Doing It

To get it right
Like a perfect cover drive
Or crosscourt backhand, or
At least to keep it simple.
To settle for what works, get
On with it, see it through
With no drama:-
This I still try for
—like Gulliver peering into
The matchbox stage with one
Huge eye, freezing the plot,
Or like him again, scuttling
Among the enormous boots.

Up Here

One by one my friends seem
To have the same thing.
Being much of an age,
We were all prone to get it.

Look at our moon faces
On their slack strings
And you see the first
Of a puckered loss.
Listen to us who are
Beginning not to listen
As our noses droop sideways
And our mouths draw in.

Among ourselves even,
Bunched together up here
We begin to be watchful,
Each hoarding what is
Left of breath.

Cocktail Party Survival Kit

What do you say to the girl,
Seventeen, with a straining shirt,
Who has just discovered Mahler?

Best of all, be called away
By the police about your wife.

Failing that, try the sort of smile
That goes sideways or in any case
Nowhere near the shirt.

If your mouth won't do the smile,
Kick one leg sharply many times
With the foot of the other leg.
Aim at a clean fracture.

While waiting for the stretcher,
On no account discuss gardens,
Apples, reptiles, or what comes
Between Mahler and Bach.

The Two Others

There are always three
And the third gets it right.
Coached by the old woman in the forest,
He answers the riddle, skewers the dragon
And claims the kingdom that
Goes with the girl.

My small son frowns.
He is always the third,
But his eye catches them, the
Twisted heap by the wall and
Something face down in the moat.

Where Were We?

In a rarely visited drawer
I find my old love hard-married
To a chocolate bar.

She wears a high chocolate hat,
Moustaches sorrowing to a patriarchal beard.
This, I remember, is what my friends were saying
And I never could admit.

Her wispy husband is not what he was.
Built for a quick clinch, short sticky pleasure,
He should have listened to his friends
And never risked a ten year kiss.

Then?

What shall I remember?
A tall gentle girl
Not sure how best to please.
Slender like a boy, a quiet grace,
Her own way of sitting, a voice
That took you to a quiet sunlit place.
And, if I dare, a lovely courtesy
Patient for love to match her love
And her own way of crying, dead quiet.
You knew only if you saw
Or felt tears on her face.

Finis

As for him,
He shakes his tray of samples,
Fetches out his winning phrases,
Plays through his repertoire.

As for her,
She mourns a thing
That wasted and died like a child.

Words mend nothing, buy back nothing.
He will need to grope,
Tap with his stick
To know this final place.

And she,
She must gather back a life,
Weave what she can of a coat
For her journey on.

Warning

In the end, propitiated or fooled or bored,
The Eumenides pack their gear and go, but,
For old time's sake, leave with us their sisters.

These, on bad days even, are never visible,
Are shy with their message, speak very quietly.
They are devoted to you-as-you-were, remember
All you said, never lose a photograph or letter.
They have no provable case, could often be answered,
But never enter court. They point rather
To the place made special in other company,
The gold held for a time and let fall.

Beware of them:
They can draw gentle hands across the sun,
Call by name each ghost you have forgotten to weep for
And turn fondly to what now you value highest.

Wording

One prayer
Is that He teach us to be ready
For that other language.

I think it would have words that
For sheer delight we dare not speak,
Words that are voyages and words
We learn infinitely slowly
Changing us as we learn them.
There would be words that are silence,
Dancing, cliffs, preludes, sheer
Surprise forgotten in the womb
And through it all present absolute,
The one endless tense.

Us

There are the three of us:
The idiot birds yelling at each other
That once more it's got light,
Me sour that I've never
Done anything worth anything
And, at the press of a button,
Wonderfully sobbing his pox-ridden
Guts out, Schubert about to
Die at thirty one.

That's about it really, except that
The birds are so totally birds,
Never wondering whether they'd
Trade in the lot to write that
Quintet or marry the girl it
Was written for or live
To see another noisy morning.

Bedside

Under her face there are others:
The strong widow glad he went quickly,
The first look at my girl, her enormous
Bedtime go to sleep, a lovely glance
From the honeymoon album, the solemn
Miss among studio roses, the sepia
Two year old with a rag elephant.

They are learning something new.
Not stop, not death, but
Night that won't be night,
Day for the hopeless luggage,
Time that comes sideways and
Jokey, tripping up the words.
Enough to clutch a hand, a toy in
The sheet, a kiss for quickly,
For go to sleep.

Interlocutory

Ah the pity of it,
Saving your Worship,
Him dying at sixty
With all that knowledge
And all that money
Squirrelled away
And a pity again
That he didn't die
And the doctors
Ridding and forbidding
And him sliding down
That way, you might say.

And the pity of it,
Saving your Honour,
Him dying at seventy
And quite a bit
He still remembered
And more's the pity
That he didn't die
Cobbled together
And the doctors
Riddling and fiddling
With their spanners
And him down most of
The way, you might say.

And the pity of it,
Saving your Grace,
Him dying at ninety
With one good eye
And half an arm left
And a pity too
He can't remember
How to die
And the doctors
Sighing and trying
To remind him
And the coffin ready
And ground all dug
For him to be out of
The way, you might say.

For You Then

Earlier than runes, earlier,
Early as firelight, old as words:
That hunting alone in the dark time,
Sun remembers Earth, turns back and
Comes to watch her waking face.

Something chanted, mimed,
Acted out in rites flecked with blood.

And after whatever, if words
Can be found in crevices
And pieced together,
It will be told again and with
The same murderous love.

For you then, you after whatever,
May it answer and may there be
The coming and the royal gentleness
And the lovely surrender.

Getting Unstraightened

Oh girls, my shadowy troupe,
Back to your airy boxes
It's time for you to go.
For lifelong passion
Which real girls never show
It's small thanks I know,
But costs run high and I must
Learn to live in frugal fashion.

Farewell Julia,
Your tigerish need, the things you said,
Your single-minded earthiness, have kept me sane
Many a night alone in bed.

Ah Jane, still shadows under your eyes I see
And still boxed in, but what times we have had
Examining your hopeless love for me.

And Teresa, virgin for ever unexplored
Despite our many married nights,
Priestess of the art of never getting bored.

You too, kinky Carla, you must go with the rest,
But cheer up, for sheer georgeous punishment
You were always by far the best.

Elsa stop snivelling, Jenny don't sulk,
Maria put down that axe,
And Lisa, Wendy, Anna, all you others . . .

Thank you for pleasure in unlikely places,
Office desk and library, airport lounge and wagon-lit,
Breathless meetings I never would have had,
Enchantment borrowed from other faces.

Shelved like this in your prime,
Believe me girls, I would not wish it so,
But costs are high and funds are low:
Back to your boxes it's time to go.

For Warmth

The stars crowd this frosty hill,
Leaning into the grass for warmth,
They too with the dark around them,
A Great Lord with time to wait,
The Lord Void who let slip
A universe from under his paw.

Keen on facts, the moon stands
A buttercup near my face
And a shadow on frost to prove it.
Jaunty head on stalk.

The stars hug branch and pylon,
They too with the Dark around them.
He is older than the stars,
Older than the thought of stars.
He outnumbers them as they
Lean into the grass for warmth.

Rue Lamargue

This early the sun will tease a wall,
Deck it with lace and bridal finery,
Hint sidelong at langour for that
Elsewhere golden time, tricking your eye
In flaxen patterns up past shutters.
This early the sun leans and idles
Out of season, tracing out a summer
As the roof-line kindles.

This early in the year the chances
Crouch like leopards and that
Bohemian room up there is yours.
You trespass high with your long hugged,
Never tried still-life of no compromise,
You unswerving for the lovely out-of-reach
And there, sketched in on the bed, the
Virgin whore who will settle what you
Are, for all your lies.

This early you might argue about
Winning and defeat and in treacherous
Paths like any leaf twisting down past
Shutters the sun can stumble.
The fishmonger stacks out his dead and
You are there among scrawls on
A door. Someone with a briefcase,
Late for a meeting, glad of a coat.

Praise Be

It seemed reasonable.
Mind would learn body's time.
They would rehearse death as a team,
Practise in step what to forget,
How to be forty, fifty,
A double act in gravitas.

And we did try, but it
Was the school pantomime;
Stuck-on beards, ill-painted
Wrinkles, bald wigs, lines
Left hanging, the ply-wood
Castle swaying, laughter
At the wrong time.

Thank heavens we do it badly.
Praise be for the under-rehearsed,
The not-forgotten, the unlearnt.
Praise all out of step, all bad
Timing, the unprompted unguarded,
Everything that shouldn't happen.

Bathing

We went bathing in a sunny backstreet,
My daughter and I. It was a room with
Sunbeams and she was flushed away
Who would now be ten.
We go bathing in the stream,
My daughter and I, her face and mine
Vague across the dazzle and the branches,
She delighting in arms and legs, the risk
Of depth, learning what sunlight is.
Always I want to get near and the water
Stands up and screams, it burns like a
Wall as she goes back behind the sun.

For What Love

For what love you have they
Sing in your head like a pulse
And the lovely answers
Come before the questions.
They argue like colour, like a dance,
Like notes in a homing arc
Thrown up for no sayable reason.
For what love, whatever love,
They are the banded snake
You were born with,
Sickness hugged close as breath,
Venom in wine of your own tillage.
They are caves, cloud-acres,
Foundries where words are made,
Your high summer of all that matters
And nothing but noises in your head.

For what love you cannot lose,
You bear their mark.
For all or nothing you sail
Your matchwood craft a mile high,
Trailing your hand in familiar wreckage,
Or they cleave rock above you
For your own crazy sun
And an inch or two of sky.

April

Just warm enough to sit and
Listen to my wall. Limestone gone
Winter-proud, stone-heavy;
Bosses and dark mouths
Gawping at the sun.

Above the door a bee probes,
Blundering in caverns
Contentedly worried, the
Loudest noise of the morning.

Pointing needed, would you say?
Or would you sit like a drunk
In an overcoat, tracing
April on your eyelids?

Music for Brass

She eager to hear and I driven at last
To a kind of honesty,
If ever there was a night for them to keep quiet,
For a silent background to the big statement,
That was it.
But there they were, barely out of sight,
Aiming to please with 'my heart for ever'
Rendered con an amore that made her giggle.

And how can I be taken seriously
If, when trouble comes, they follow me
Single file, genuine ex-service disabled
—God bless you Guvnor—
With a funeral march blown a quarter tone flat?

And of course when things go right,
The occasion for simple joy,
They are happy too and wear funny hats
And—Oompah Oompah—I get waggish numbers,
Bumslapped lederhosen up an Alp.

They've been with me for years.
My friends complain and so do I,
But where else would they get a job?
And, to be truthful, I am used to their noise
And would miss them if they went.